P9-DFC-692

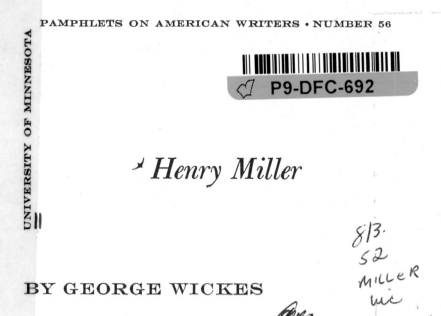

Henry Miller

BY GEORGE WICKES

813.
52
MILLER
wic

FINKELSTEIN
MEMORIAL LIBRARY
SPRING VALLEY, N. Y.

UNIVERSITY OF MINNESOTA PRESS · MINNEAPOLIS

860352 PAPER

© Copyright 1966 by the University of Minnesota

ALL RIGHTS RESERVED

Printed in the United States of America at
the North Central Publishing Company, St. Paul

Library of Congress Catalog Card Number: 66-63488

Distributed to high schools in the United States by Webster Division
McGraw-Hill Book Company
St. Louis   New York   San Francisco   Dallas

PUBLISHED IN GREAT BRITAIN, INDIA, AND PAKISTAN BY THE OXFORD
UNIVERSITY PRESS, LONDON, BOMBAY, AND KARACHI, AND IN CANADA
BY THE COPP CLARK PUBLISHING CO. LIMITED, TORONTO

HENRY MILLER

GEORGE WICKES teaches at Harvey Mudd College and Claremont Graduate School. He has edited *Lawrence Durrell and Henry Miller: A Private Correspondence, Henry Miller and the Critics,* and an interview of Henry Miller which appeared in the *Paris Review.*

⤴ *Henry Miller*

Henry Miller is likely to outlast a great many writers who at the moment seem more important. Fifty years from now, a hundred years from now, he will remain a significant figure of our time. The future will remember him for a variety of reasons, not all of them literary. For Henry Miller is not only a writer, he is a phenomenon. His life, his creed, his motives, and his work are all of interest to an enormous public. He is venerated by an extraordinary number of people at home and abroad, not all of them cranks by any means. His name is news and is bound to become history. He epitomizes a movement, a trend, perhaps a revolution in mores. To many he represents a cause. For such reasons his work and reputation are as difficult to appraise now as were those of Rousseau and Byron in their day. Like them he should probably be viewed first as a public figure, and only then as a writer.

Most conspicuously, Henry Miller is the man who broke the barriers on what is loosely called pornography, whose books won test cases and made certain words printable in English-speaking countries. *Tropic of Cancer*, first published overtly in this country in 1961, soon became the subject of more widespread litigation than any other literary work in history and eventually required a Supreme Court decision. The controversy stirred up by *Ulysses* and *Lady Chatterley's Lover* was mild by comparison — though in England the trial of Lady Chatterley had already established precedent and Miller's works have consequently appeared there without challenge.

The publication of *Tropic of Cancer* in America created a furore, with some sixty lawsuits waged in different states. It was also an enormous success, with 1,500,000 copies sold within a year, and another 1,000,000 the following year. Thus almost thirty years after he had written the book Henry Miller became a best seller in his native land, and after many years of poverty a rich man. *Tropic of Cancer* was followed by *Tropic of Capricorn* in 1962, and *Black Spring* in 1963. Then in 1965, all the other banned books appeared at once: *The World of Sex, Quiet Days in Clichy*, and the three volumes of *The Rosy Crucifixion, Sexus, Plexus,* and *Nexus*. These books had previously been published in France and had occasionally appeared in America in small editions sold illicitly, usually by dealers in erotica.

The publication of Miller's books would make an interesting study in itself. There have been hundreds of editions and translations all over the world, a good share of them pirated. The history of his authorized publications might be briefly summed up in the names of a few publishers: Jack Kahane of the Obelisk Press in Paris, who specialized in pornography for the tourist trade, published Miller's first five books; James Laughlin of New Directions, champion of experimental writing, introduced Miller to American readers; Bern Porter, who ran a private press in the forties, was one of the many who printed fugitive Milleriana; Maurice Girodias of Olympia Press, son and successor of Jack Kahane, was prosecuted and sentenced by the French government for publishing, among other works, *Sexus*; and most recently, Barney Rosset of Grove Press has forced acceptance of the banned books in the United States. All have taken up Miller as a cause and professed the highest motives in publishing his works; all have taken risks in doing so, but only Girodias has suffered seriously. Laughlin has probably been the most disinterested, Rosset certainly the most successful in establishing Miller in the marketplace. The industry of private publishers like Bern Porter has produced a great variety of miscellaneous ephemera, pamphlets for the most part drawn from Miller's books, which have become collector's items and which have complicated the bibliographer's task.

During the years when he was struggling for recognition Miller became a legendary character, a kind of folk hero, the Paul Bunyan of literature, larger than life as exile, bohemian, and rebel, the great champion of freedom of expression and other lost causes. He appealed to highbrows and lowbrows alike, although in the early years his admirers were not always able to obtain his works. He gained a good deal of sympathy in 1943 when the *New Republic* published his open letters begging for food, clothing, or cash and offering watercolors in exchange. This campaign was so successful — in spreading his reputation at least — that later when the GI's in France began buying up copies of his *Tropics* at a great rate and his financial problems were solved, his name remained a byword for the plight of the creative artist in America.

When he settled in Big Sur, on an isolated stretch of the California coast, the place became famous. His legend grew, and strange stories circulated about the Henry Miller "cult," most of them sensational and false. Pilgrims came to visit Miller from all parts of the country and abroad, so many that eventually he had to leave. It is characteristic of America and this day of public images that Miller should still be identified as the monkish Sage of Big Sur, while the place, once a colony for poor writers and artists, should be transformed into a fashionable resort. It is surely more significant that his example has had a profound effect on many writers and artists the world over, among whom he is venerated as a free spirit. And the lengthened shadow of the man is most apparent in the fact that he is the original beatnik and Zen saint — in this as in so many other ways thirty years ahead of his followers.

Miller has also played a conspicuous public role as outsider, rebel, and iconoclast. He is in fact a genuine anarchist, a con-

7

firmed enemy of society, constitutionally opposed to any system. Miller's position has a long tradition in America. His anarchy derives from the individualism of his heroes, Emerson, Thoreau, and Whitman, the latter in Miller's opinion "the greatest man America ever produced." Similarly his anti-Americanism, though cultivated abroad, is of the homegrown variety, and in latter years, without abating his vehement criticism of America, he has gone so far as to confess that he is 100 per cent American. At first his iconoclasm appears to be a product of the thirties; doubtless he will be remembered by historians as a voice out of the Great Depression, a writer of protest. But though his early works are wonderfully expressive of that era, the depression atmosphere has nothing to do with the thirties. Henry Miller had been living in the depression all his life; the depression mentality is to be found throughout his work, and in his autobiographical narratives can be traced back to his childhood. He was always a bottom dog in spirit, always an outsider, always — to use one of his favorite words — a bedbug.

Perhaps the best way to view him is as a writer of satire. If we can accept John Dos Passos' definition, "A satirist is a man whose flesh creeps so at the ugly and the savage and the incongruous aspects of society that he has to express them as brutally and nakedly as possible to get relief." Much of Dos Passos' essay on "Satire as a Way of Seeing," though written for George Grosz's drawings, applies with remarkable aptness to Miller's writings. "He seeks to put his grisly obsession into expressive form the way a bacteriologist seeks to isolate a virus. . . . Instead of letting you be the superior bystander laughing in an Olympian way at somebody absurd, [he] makes you identify yourself with the sordid and pitiful object. His satire hurts." If Miller is indeed a satirist, then he belongs to a very special breed. He has the satirist's usual irreverence, but none of his indignation. Though appalled at the world

8

around him and despairing of its future, he is not depressed but elated by the spectacle. He has been profoundly affected by Spengler, yet is full of high spirits. He dances with glee as the world goes to pieces. His pessimism is that of the satirist, but his comic despair is *sui generis*.

Whether or not Miller can be regarded as a satirist, there can be no doubt about what he is against. He is radically anti-bourgeois, anti-white-Nordic-Protestant, and, as already noted, anti-American. He is utterly opposed to the bourgeois ethic of work and wealth. To him Christianity is bankrupt, the American dream a nightmare. What he hates most in America is the utilitarian cult of progress, efficiency, and the machine, all of which he sees as dehumanizing, soul-destroying forces. He is anti-Utopian because he does not believe in economic or political solutions. He is anti-civilization, to such a point that "civilization" is a dirty word in his vocabulary. "Civilization is drugs, alcohol, engines of war, prostitution, machines and machine slaves, low wages, bad food, bad taste, prisons, reformatories, lunatic asylums, divorce, perversion, brutal sports, suicides, infanticide, cinema, quackery, demagogy, strikes, lockouts, revolutions, putsches, colonization, electric chairs, guillotines, sabotage, floods, famine, disease, gangsters, money barons, horse racing, fashion shows, poodle dogs, chow dogs, Siamese cats, condoms, pessaries, syphilis, gonorrhea, insanity, neuroses, etc., etc." This definition makes him sound more like a prophet of doom than a merry-andrew, but it is precisely such a collection of horrors that will touch off his gaiety.

Although Miller is anything but a coherent thinker, his attitudes are all of a piece. They recur throughout his work, consistent from start to finish. In his attitudes he is a close successor to D. H. Lawrence; his experiences have led him to Lawrence's conclusions. He shares Lawrence's vision of humanity being ground apart by the machine; his response closely resembles that of Lawrence,

Dionysian, anti-intellectual, instinctive; he turns to the same life-giving sources, art, religion, and sex. To use a favorite term of contemporary criticism, both are prophetic, apocalyptic writers. Here the resemblance ends. Temperamentally the two are altogether different, as different as tragedy and comedy. Where Lawrence is inclined to play the messiah, Miller prefers to play the clown.

Art, religion, and sex. Miller is easily recognized as an apostle of art and sex, but the religious element may be harder to detect in his work. By conventional standards he is immoral, profane, and blasphemous. He is not pious, virtuous, solemn, puritanical, dogmatic, or orthodox — he has none of the attributes that Americans usually associate with religion, and he clearly has no use for them. Yet Miller regards himself as a religious man, frequently mentions God in his work, and readily alludes to such religious figures as Gautama, Jesus, and, his favorite, Lao-tse. What he means by God and religion is often hard to determine, because he is so completely eclectic in his views. Often in his early works, God means simply the divine afflatus or self-fulfillment. And religion, especially in his later works, can include anything that might loosely be labeled mysticism or metaphysics. Miller has always been attracted to all kinds of exotic and esoteric systems, such as astrology, theosophy, and occultism. In rejecting organized Christianity, he did not close his mind to religion, but rather opened it to all manner of unconventional para-religious beliefs, preferably Oriental in origin. And in religion as in everything else he remains a hedonist, an anarchist, and a humorist; this combination makes it particularly difficult for more conventional minds to accept Miller as a religious person.

Sex is of course the most controversial element in his work; it assumes many forms and serves many purposes. Sometimes it is purely gratuitous, mere bawdy storytelling, but at other times it is symbolic. At its most meaningful sex serves as the most powerful weapon against the system he is attacking. It is the life-force, the only force that can rescue man from the machine. Here again Miller resembles Lawrence; but he does not go on with Lawrence to develop a mystique of sex. With him sex is usually casual, carnal, anarchic, and indiscriminate. In writing about it, he is crude, blunt, explicit. Worse still, he uses the everyday words that he learned in the streets as a boy.

These words are still explosive in print. It is probably Miller's language more than anything else that aroused the censors, and still makes it exceedingly difficult to debate the pornography-obscenity issue dispassionately. There is also a problem of definition, and in the lawcourts a question of the writer's intent. Miller cheerfully admits that he is an obscene writer, but claims not to be a pornographer. He bases his distinction largely on candor: obscenity to him is direct, while pornography is suggestive. Pornography might be described simply as aphrodisiac, obscenity as disgusting. Pornography is romantic, making sex appear more alluring than it actually is; while obscenity, to the contrary, makes sex repulsive or ridiculous. By now no one challenges Miller's motives much; certainly he did not write about sex to make money — he is not a pornographer in that sense. In time the whole issue is likely to appear ludicrous, a quaint episode in a changing cultural pattern. After all, pornography has flourished mainly in a few puritanical countries during the last two hundred years or less; elsewhere and at other times, sex has almost invariably been regarded as comical. Already there are signs that the English-speaking peoples are growing less squeamish about reading the dozen or so words that make up the obscene vocabulary. If so, Henry Miller has been largely responsible for their acceptance in print.

As might be expected, Miller is as iconoclastic on the subject of literature as on any other subject. He constantly argues that what he is writing is not literature, for "literary," like "civilization," is a nasty word in his vocabulary. What he objects to chiefly in literature is "the insufferable, the obsessional lucidity of the mind" in such writers as Proust, Joyce, Pound, and Eliot, the "mortuary odor" of form and tradition. To these analytical writers he opposes Rimbaud, Dostoevski, and D. H. Lawrence. Literature should be written entirely from the subconscious, not from the head. It should flow spontaneously, it should not be concerned with form. "The terrible emphasis today upon plot, action, character, analysis, etc. — all this false emphasis which characterizes the literature and drama of our day — simply reveals the lack of these elements in our life." Such statements show what he had in mind when he wrote his own books: he would re-create life as he lived it.

For all his anti-literary protest, Miller has plenty of literary ancestors. His very intransigence belongs to a venerable tradition, that of the literary underworld. As a literary outlaw, he is the descendant of such writers as Petronius, Villon, Rabelais, Balzac, and Lautréamont, all the rogues and picaros and *poètes maudits*, as well as the ancestors previously mentioned. By now he is well on the way to becoming an ancestor himself, with numerous descendants. Though inadequately recognized, his influence is perhaps the most pervasive in American writing today. Such dissimilar writers as Burroughs and Kerouac, Mailer and Baldwin, are in their different ways indebted to Miller, and the Beats have hailed him as a precursor. To a remarkable degree, the present generation of American writers has inherited his traits: egocentric and confessional; shocking, violent, obscene; rambling, incoherent, formless; antisocial, anarchic, solipsistic; "mystical"; hallucinatory, nightmarish, ecstatic, apocalyptic.

The explanation for Miller's extreme individualism can be found in his biography: briefly, he is a self-made man. Self-educated, formed by his experiences, slow to mature and self-taught as a writer, he struggled for years before he broke through with *Tropic of Cancer,* by which time his opinions were fully formed. Self-made in the Emersonian sense, he was as intransigent as Thoreau, the American he most resembles, once due allowance is made for the differences in character and setting: Miller is neither disciplined nor ascetic, and the streets of megalopolis were his Harvard and Walden. An account of his first forty years shows that he constantly rebelled against the standards of his society, formed his own, and lived by them as much as possible. During much of his life he has lived marginally. In a country where work is synonymous with virtue, he has seldom held a steady job and has preferred the hand-to-mouth existence of a beggar or bum. He has knocked about a good deal, working at one time or other as "dish-washer, bus boy, newsie, messenger boy, grave-digger, bill sticker, book salesman, bell hop, bartender, liquor salesman, typist, adding machine operator, librarian, statistician, charity worker, mechanic, insurance collector, garbage collector, usher, secretary to an evangelist, dock hand, street car conductor, gymnasium instructor, milk driver, ticket chopper, etc." Thoreau too worked at odd jobs.

Miller's employment record is taken from the "Autobiographical Note" written in 1939 for *The Cosmological Eye,* the book which introduced him to American readers. That note and the Chronology appended to *The Henry Miller Reader* twenty years later provide the best objective account of Miller's life. Subjective accounts appear all through his writings, but the facts are often romanticized, warped, and otherwise colored for the particular effect he seeks. The "Autobiographical Note" is not only brief and factual; it also provides a sort of *apologia pro vita sua* that helps one to understand the motives behind Miller's life and writings. "My grandfathers came to America to escape military service. . . . From five to ten were the most important years of my life; I lived in the street and acquired the typical American gangster spirit. . . . The Spanish-American war, which broke out when I was seven, was a big event in my young life; I enjoyed the mob spirit which broke loose and which permitted me to understand at an early age the violence and lawlessness which is so characteristic of America. . . . I had no desire to earn a living, no sense of economy, and no respect for my elders or for laws or institutions. I defied my parents and those about me almost from the time I was able to talk."

Miller's work is full of his boyhood memories of Brooklyn and his later experiences in New York City. Born in the Yorkville section of New York on December 26, 1891, he grew up in Brooklyn, went to school there, and to this day retains much of his Brooklyn accent. As a young man he often crossed Brooklyn Bridge to Manhattan, where his father had a tailor shop. Until 1930 New York was his home. "I am a city man through and through; I hate nature, just as I hate the 'classics.'" Of his early years Miller has written most lyrically in two sections of *Black Spring*, "The Fourteenth Ward" and "The Tailor Shop." The world he depicts is not the "American" New York of Whitman or Edith Wharton, but the immigrant melting pot with its teeming neighborhoods, all redolent of the old country. In this polyglot world Miller learned to speak German before English and grew up with the sound of Yiddish and Polish in his ears. As a boy he ran wild in the streets, while his father moved in a comfortable masculine atmosphere of bars and good eating, with the easy comradeship of actors, salesmen, and other sporting types. In his prime Henry's father appears to have been gregarious, easygoing, and bibulous; later Henry nostalgically envied his father's way of life. Henry's mother, who was rigidly conventional, seems to have inspired the rebel in him; he never had a kind word to say of her. There was a streak of insanity in the family, amusingly represented in Tante Melia, pathetically in Henry's sister.

The best insight into his family background is provided in "Reunion in Brooklyn," written when Miller returned home after ten years abroad and regarded his family with a cold eye. A marvel of restraint, it nevertheless compels sympathy and horror, as Miller is forced to witness the helplessness of his grotesquely dying father domineered by a compulsive, niggardly wife. The result is a merciless portrayal of American family life with all its monstrous middle-class virtues. The son himself plays his part in this parable of the middle-aged prodigal and feels twinges of bourgeois remorse. Like many artists in America, Miller had to combat not only public opinion but his own sense of shame, ingrained despite his better judgment, at having failed to earn money. In *Black Spring* Miller writes, "In the past every member of our family did something with his hands. I'm the first idle son of a bitch with a glib tongue and a bad heart." But elsewhere he says there were poets and musicians among his German ancestors.

His formal education ended soon after high school. He enrolled at City College of New York but, unable to stand the academic routine, only stayed for about two months. Then for a period of ten years or more, he worked at a great variety of jobs, never for any length of time, and drifted across the country and back. During this time he also trained strenuously, both in athletics and music. He writes of velocity exercises at the piano and training for the Olympics — figuratively perhaps, but his furious energy suggests a creative drive frenetically seeking expression. He continued his education on his own, reading, attending lectures, talking with famous or unknown persons. His autobiographical notes are full of momentous encounters, such as: "Met Emma Goldman in San

Diego: turning point in life." Or "Met with Robert Hamilton Challacombe of the Theosophical Society, Point Loma, California. Decisive event. Led to meeting with Benjamin Fay Mills, ex-evangelist." But chiefly he read. Voraciously and indiscriminately he absorbed works on a wide range of subjects. And he read with the autodidact's sense of discovery, oblivious to received opinion. The result, recorded in *The Books in My Life*, proves a rather erratic liberal education, with emphasis on Oriental mysticism and adventure fiction. Here Belloc and Madame Blavatsky rub elbows with Nietzsche and Spengler. The last two probably affected his thinking more than any other writers. His first serious effort at writing was an essay on Nietzsche's *Antichrist*. He wrote it on the job, in his father's tailor shop, according to one account, or when he was working for a mail-order house, according to another; in the latter version he was caught by the boss and fired forthwith. Whichever is true, he was obviously more interested in Nietzsche than in business.

In 1920, already a married man and a father, he settled down to a steady job for almost five years. In the best American tradition he began at the bottom, but after a few months' apprenticeship he was at the top, as employment manager of Western Union in New York City. Incredibly enough, he was just the man for that position. The whole story demonstrates Miller's extraordinary ability to charm people with words. With a mixture of brashness and persuasion that any salesman would envy, he demanded an interview with the president of the company, and was promptly hired for a highly responsible position, though he had to serve as a messenger first to get acquainted with the system. So the story goes in *Tropic of Capricorn*, and there is no reason to doubt it. The man who hired Miller must have sized up his particular gifts, his quick perception, his ability to manage people, his essential toughness. It was a heartbreaking job. Every day he had to inter-

16

view, hire, and fire messengers, sometimes by the hundreds — a total, he claims, of 100,000 in five years. All forms of human life passed by him every day, mostly the desperate and derelict. They educated him in anguish and cynicism; they made him hard-boiled and compassionate. Hence the attitude that pervades his work. If he had any illusions about the system before, he lost them all now. The experience opened his eyes forever. "It was a slaughterhouse, so help me God. The thing was senseless from the bottom up. A waste of men, material and effort. A hideous farce against a backdrop of sweat and misery. . . . The whole system was so rotten, so inhuman, so lousy, so hopelessly corrupt and complicated, that it would have taken a genius to put any sense or order into it, to say nothing of human kindness or consideration." Not only *Tropic of Capricorn* but all of Miller's books are informed by this view.

One day the vice-president of Western Union suggested to Miller that someone should write a book about the messengers. What he had in mind was a Horatio Alger story, but the idea that seized Miller was altogether different. Suddenly he saw the opportunity to vent his fury against the company and the American dream. "I was determined to wipe Horatio Alger out of the North American consciousness." In 1922, he sat down and wrote his first book during a three-week vacation. "Clipped Wings" was the story of twelve Western Union messengers. The manuscript has disappeared, but some idea of its contents can be gathered from *Tropic of Capricorn*, where Miller briefly recapitulates five case histories. The characters are out of Dostoevski, gentle souls, insulted and injured, who run amok or suffer violence; the stories are full of bitterness and horror, ending in murder or suicide, usually both. Miller confesses that the book was a hopeless failure because he knew nothing about writing and could not cope with such overwhelming material. But it gave him the urge to go on writing.

In 1924 he quit Western Union, resolved never to take another job and determined to become a writer. As a matter of fact he worked again at many jobs, for it took him ten years to get published and he was often hungry. During this time he wrote three novels that have remained in manuscript, "Moloch," "Crazy Cock," and "This Gentile World," in addition to many shorter works. Emulating Whitman he peddled his prose-poems from door to door. By this time he had divorced his first wife and married the femme fatale of his autobiographical works. A taxi dancer with intellectual aspirations, she encouraged him to write and supported him financially. She also deployed her charms in selling his prose-poems, sometimes signed with her name. In 1928 she found the money which permitted them to spend a year in Europe. That trip opened up a new world for Miller. He had been oriented toward European culture as a young man by Emma Goldman, and more recently by his boyhood friend, Emil Schnellock, a painter who had spent several years abroad. But he was still a provincial, Europe was still a romantic dream, and he went there as a tourist — in the same frame of mind as most Americans traveling in Europe in the twenties. Two years later he returned there to live. His wife was to join him and did in fact make several brief visits to Paris, but their separation ended in divorce, and for the next fifteen years Miller led the bachelor existence recorded in *Tropic of Cancer* and other books. Miller's autobiographical accounts are full of decisive moments, but unquestionably his return to Paris in 1930 marked the turning point in his life. Only there and then was he able to complete the metamorphosis that would make him a writer. He stayed there until 1939 and might never have left if the war had not forced him to return to America.

It is hard to imagine Miller without Paris. French culture suited him as no other would have done; it liberated him and permeated him, satisfying his psychic and artistic needs. In Paris he wrote his best books and found a publisher willing to take them. Oddly enough, he settled there by chance, or as he would have it, Paris was in his horoscope; he had intended to go to Madrid but ran out of money and never got any farther than Paris. But Paris promptly became his city and his way of life. During his first two years there he lived from hand to mouth, but starving in Paris was incomparably better than starving in New York and provided him with a wealth of new material. He lived largely by his charm. With his faculty for making friends and his great conversational gifts, he soon found fourteen people willing to feed him a meal a week in exchange for his company. Generous himself to a point of prodigality, he never hesitated to accept the generosity of others. After two years, he moved into an apartment with Alfred Perlès, a writer and kindred spirit. For two and a half years they lived together in the ugly proletarian district of Clichy and they continued the greatest of friends until 1938, when Perlès migrated to London. These were the happiest and most productive years of Miller's life.

In his writings Miller has no doubt exaggerated his sufferings. The real misery was not being published. Yet he could not give up; the demon within him demanded expression. He had brought his latest manuscript with him to Paris, but there again met discouragement. Finally in desperation he decided to write as he pleased — not for the publishers but for himself. Since no one would publish what he wrote anyway, he was free to write in his own fashion. Up to this point his writing had been "literary," that is, derivative. Now he found his own voice. In the fall of his second year in Paris he began to write *Tropic of Cancer*. It was not published until 1934, but Miller was a writer at last.

Miller writes in two main genres. His work is about evenly divided between narrative and expository modes. He is best known for his narrative works, such as the early *Tropics*. Critics have usually treated these books as novels, because Miller's method is that of fiction, but he has always insisted that he is writing autobiography or "autobiographical romances." They might best be described as confessions and the method as picaresque. They are confessions in Rousseau's sense of the word, introspective, autobiographical monologues; like Rousseau, Miller is usually trying to argue a thesis from his personal experience.

The expository writings are harder to classify. They would usually be defined as essays, but they assume a variety of forms: letters, criticism, travel, portraiture, anecdote, reminiscence, opinion. The personal essay admits plenty of latitude, which Miller has taken, incorporating a good deal of narrative technique. The essays represent Miller in his shorter flights and most commonly serve as a vehicle for his ideas, or rather opinions. Most of them were originally written for periodicals and later collected for publication in book form. Miller himself has no use for literary genres — or literary criticism for that matter. To him all of his work expresses a man.

The richest period of Miller's writing career is also the most varied. This is the period he spent in Paris and its immediate aftermath. In a volcanic creative outburst, he produced stories, articles, books, at the rate of a volume a year. During this decade he wrote the three picaresque narratives generally regarded as his best and most characteristic works, *Tropic of Cancer, Black Spring,* and *Tropic of Capricorn.* He also wrote two books in epistolary form, *Aller Retour New York* and *Hamlet,* the latter in collaboration with Michael Fraenkel. At the same time he worked on a study of D. H. Lawrence; edited a zany little magazine; published books by his friends; wrote several stray pamphlets and enough articles and stories to fill two miscellanies, *Max and the White Phagocytes* and *The Wisdom of the Heart.* Upon his return to New York in 1940 he wrote a manifesto, *The World of Sex*; the two narratives that constitute *Quiet Days in Clichy*; and an account of his visit to Greece in 1939, *The Colossus of Maroussi*.

Of all his books *Tropic of Cancer* (1934) gave him the most trouble. Although the manuscript was promptly accepted by the Obelisk Press, its publication was deferred for more than two years. Meanwhile Miller rewrote it three times. Neither his struggle nor the publisher's delay is surprising. Miller had to learn how to write all over again, and Jack Kahane had to calculate the risk of publishing a violently obscene book. He took a copy of the manuscript around to various colleagues in the publishing world to sound out his chances. They were impressed by the book, but felt that it could never be published, even in France, where few people read English and censorship was virtually nonexistent. The book was probably improved by the delay, which kept Miller revising and gave him plenty of opportunity to practice his new mode of expression.

Tropic of Cancer is an account of the adventures and encounters of an American in Paris. Written in the first person and the present tense, it conveys a strong sense of the speaking voice and the continuing moment. The narrator is named Henry Miller, and the technique is basically interior monologue, reporting successive states of mind and sensation as they occur, with all the fragmentary nature of the true stream of consciousness: a hodgepodge of incidents, memories, hallucinations, sights, ruminations, conversations, nightmares. There are frequent interruptions and shifts, back and forth in time, or altogether out of time into dream and fantasy. The disorder is intentional. Miller wanted "to get off the gold standard of literature," to write as he spoke, and to revise nothing that he had written. Behind his bewildering technique there is some organization, however; the structure is roughly chronological, with distinct episodes succeeding each other and following the calendar from autumn to summer. The book is also divided into chapters, unnumbered and untitled, but each with a theme. Then there is the overriding theme of "cancer and delirium." These organizing principles are not readily apparent; the first impression created by the book is one of chaos, with the first chapter the most chaotic. In fact the uninitiated reader is likely to miss the underlying themes altogether, for what is far more striking at first is Miller's intention to record "all that which is omitted in books." The reaction of many readers is shock; others are unimpressed by Miller's attempt to shock; still others are bored. But those who can accept the obscenity calmly may begin to find meaning behind it.

"The world is a cancer eating itself away." If the whole system is cancerous, even radical surgery is futile. Miller finds cancer in all the vital parts, in religion and art as well as politics and war. The whole modern world is an obscenity, compared to which his obscenity is wholesome. Miller offers no hope, no cure; he is not a reformer. He merely presents a picture of the world as he sees it, full of depravity, disease, filth. Through squalid scenes and characters he presents a repulsive view of humanity. Yet, far from being disgusted himself, he is delighted with squalor; he wallows in the lower depths. His response to cancer and delirium is obscenity and comedy.

The two central chapters, the crudest and funniest in the book, offer perhaps the best examples. One presents Miller's impressions of India through three despicable creatures: his employer (a truly Petronian touch of self-irony!), Mr. Nonentity, with his pearls and his prayers and withered arm clearly representing the wealth of the Indies, its religious mumbo jumbo and its impotence; Kepi, the parasite, lecher, and pimp; and the disciple of Gandhi, forgetting his holy mission in dissipation, and committing a faux pas that outrages the gentility of a brothel. Miller exhibits no veneration for the mystical, mysterious Orient here. On the contrary, he shows all that is venal, contemptible, sordid — and ludicrous. Yet from these three clowns he intuits three marvelous perceptions: a Keatsian vision of India's godlike temple sculptures rising out of this frail flesh; a profound awareness of India's staggering problems and despair at their (American) solution, plumbing, machinery, and efficiency; and finally, in a reverie proceeding from Gandhi to Gautama and Jesus, a devastating recognition of man's dunghill existence. He reaches the rockbottom of disillusionment here, but is emancipated in the process: ". . . suddenly, inspired by the absolute hopelessness of everything, I felt relieved . . . nothing had been destroyed except my illusions. I myself was intact. . . . henceforth I would live as an animal, a beast of prey, a rover, a plunderer. . . . Physically I am alive. Morally I am free."

The next chapter offers a key to much of the sex and obscenity in Miller's writing. By far the longest chapter in *Tropic of Cancer*, it deals with a number of subjects, centered around the amours of Van Norden and Carl, two of Henry Miller's friends. Van Norden is obsessed with sex. It is he and not the author who overuses the four-letter words in his monotonous monologues. Henry Miller as usual is the amused listener and spectator. With a detachment that is downright scientific he watches Van Norden engage in sex with a pitiful hungry prostitute, a mechanical act without meaning: "It's like watching one of those crazy machines which throw the newspaper out, millions and billions and trillions of them with their meaningless headlines. The machine seems more sensible, crazy as it is, and more fascinating to watch, than the human beings and the events which produced it. . . . As long as that spark of passion is missing there is no human significance in the performance." The newspaper is another important symbol in this chapter, bringing together the horrors and inanities of the modern world, but the central conjunction is money and sex. Carl's affair with a rich woman complements Van Norden's bout with the prostitute; the roles are reversed, with Carl selling his services. Miller is sometimes sentimental about prostitutes, but not here. To give oneself for money is not only meaningless but debasing. Miller values passion and despises money. The chapter ends with a rhapsody on the paintings of Matisse which make human flesh eternally beautiful. Only in the world of art does man escape from money and machinery.

Black Spring, published in 1936, two years after *Tropic of Cancer,* deals with many of the same themes, but in a different mood. "I am Chancre, the crab, which moves sideways and backwards and forwards at will. I move in strange tropics," Miller announces, explaining the connection between this and the earlier book. And the black spring of the title is another metaphor of the world's blight. But he is less fierce now, less hungry, more euphoric. There is less sex and obscenity, less action and violence. Instead of taking place only in the immediate present, the narrative moves in time and place, from Paris to memories of Brooklyn and New York and on to other planes, to reverie and fantasia. There is more delirium than cancer now, more dream, hallucination, and schizophrenia, as Miller explores different modes and levels of perception. The subject of *Black Spring* is really the imagination in all its forms, especially the creative imagination.

Each of its ten self-contained sections is an exercise in a different medium of art or the imagination, or in several media. "The Angel Is My Watermark!" for instance investigates literary inspiration, the vision of the mad, and watercolor technique. It begins with Miller possessed by "the dictation" that goes on in his head, beyond his control. He can only write down what is being dictated to him until finally it ceases, leaving him exhausted. He then turns to a fascinating book on art and insanity, which prompts him to do a watercolor. The rest of the piece explains how a watercolor happens, through a process as fortuitous as his writing. "When you're an *instinctive* water-colorist everything happens according to God's will."

Another selection ("Into the Night Life . . .") is the scenario of a nightmare. Vividly pictorial, it is like a surrealist film, full of irrational sequences, screaming terrors, Freudian guilt and logic. Like any good nightmare it is experienced: one is there, being pursued, unable to run, locked in, frantically trying to find a way out. The world tilts and the scene shifts constantly in this "Coney Island of the mind," where memories are jumbled together with Gothic visions in a world of crazy symbols that make sense.

Miller has written a great deal about the creative process elsewhere, but never so effectively. *Black Spring* demonstrates the creative imagination at work on all levels. "In ordinary waking life," Miller explains in his surrealistic vocabulary, "the author suffers from normal vision but in the frontispiece he renders himself myopic in order to grasp the immediacy of the dream plasm. By means of the dream technique he peels off the outer layers of his geologic mortality and comes to grips with his true mantic self, a non-stratified area of semi-liquid character. Only the amorphous side of his nature now possesses validity. By submerging the visible I he dives below the threshold of his schizophrenic habit patterns. He swims joyously, ad lib., in the amniotic fluid, one with his amoebic self." Miller believes that writing should be as spontaneous and unconscious as possible. Hence his own writing is full of free association and improvisation. There are passages of automatic writing — cadenzas, he sometimes calls them — when the dictation possesses him. Miller at the typewriter is like a centaur; he becomes one with the machine, and works in furious bursts. The result is a succession of discontinuous virtuoso passages that show where he sat down to write and where he left off.

Stylistically *Black Spring* is a dazzling book, the work of a rampant imagination intoxicated with words. Miller is a poet of reckless abandon, his language exuberant and prodigal, often used for sound rather than meaning. Fond of jargon and parody, he readily spins off into nonsense and jabberwocky. "Jabberwhorl Cronstadt," a verbal caricature of a friend, parodies his multisyllabic pontification and turns it into nonsense. During the course of his conversation, Jabberwhorl grows progressively drunk, and the language reels: " '. . . the great vertiginous vertebration . . . the zoospores and the leucocytes . . . the wamroths and the holenlindens. . . . every one's a poem. The jellyfish is a poem too — the finest kind of poem. You poke him here, you poke him there, he slithers and slathers, he's dithy and clabberous, he has a colon and intestines, he's vermiform and ubisquishous.' "

As that final pun indicates, Jabberwhorl's jellyfish is descended from James Joyce as well as Lewis Carroll. "Jabberwhorl Cronstadt," indeed the whole of *Black Spring*, is full of Joycean passages. Like the great parodist Miller writes not in one style, but in many. Not only is each section of *Black Spring* written in a different style, but individual sections are written in a chameleon style that borrows its constantly changing colors from a dozen sources. Besides Joyce the authors he most frequently resembles are Proust and Whitman. Like the *Tropics*, *Black Spring* is Proustian in its view of coexistent time and place stimulated by memory and the senses; Miller's writing is evocative and nostalgic. His affinity to Whitman is more fundamental, for Whitman contributes to his stance as well as his style. "For me the book is the man," Miller declares, "and my book is the man I am, the confused man, the negligent man, the reckless man, the lusty, obscene, boisterous, thoughtful, scrupulous, lying, diabolically truthful man that I am." Miller's rhetoric is like Whitman's, with long rhythmic lines

26

pulsing along through present participles. His description of the Seine could be scanned as Whitmanesque verse:

> . . . this still jet rushing on from out of a million
>   billion roots,
> this still mirror bearing the clouds along and
>   stifling the past,
> rushing on and on and on while between the mirror
>   and the clouds moving transversally
> I, a complete corporate entity,
> a universe bringing countless centuries to a
>   conclusion,
> I and this that passes beneath me
> and this that floats above me
> and all that surges through me . . .

Like Whitman too, Miller is fond of catalogues. *Black Spring* is full of them. One catalogue of American names runs on for two full pages, recapitulating the American scene from American Can to the Banks of the Wabash.

Tropic of Capricorn (1939), the third of Miller's personal narratives, is more strictly autobiographical. Whereas *Tropic of Cancer* portrayed the author-narrator living in the eternal creative present, *Tropic of Capricorn* goes back to the years before he had discovered himself as a writer. In trying to explain how and why he became a writer he reviews more than thirty years of his past experience. He succeeds mainly in conveying his sense of alienation from American life. Capricorn, the sign of the zodiac, symbolizes his destiny and complements the rich symbolism of cancer. For cancer is not only the symbol of disease and corruption, it is also the zodiacal sign of the poet and the versatile, maneuverable crab. "Opposite Cancer in the zodiac (extremes of the Equinox — turning points) is Capricorn," Miller wrote in a letter to Anaïs Nin at the time he was finishing his second *Tropic*, "the house in which I am born, which is religious and represents renaissance in death.

Cancer also means for me the disease of civilization, the extreme point of realization along the wrong path — hence the necessity to change one's course and begin all over again." Hence too the dominant theme of resurrection which runs all through the work, in many images of suffering, death, and revival as well as more explicit allusion. Miller is most explicit when he examines his horoscope. Born too late, on December 26 instead of the day before, he was nevertheless "born with a crucifixion complex. . . . born a fanatic." He has experienced crucifixion and resurrection in several forms: he has gone "beyond the sense of desperation and futility," beyond tragedy and survived, but transformed; he has gone "through too great love" and been born again; and though he does not say so explicitly in *Tropic of Capricorn*, it was in his thirty-third year that he quit Western Union in order to be reborn a writer. Such experiences have carried him beyond human suffering to the point of detachment and gaiety. He is a man who has been to the bottom and risen again, purged of his feelings. But his literary model is not so much Dante's *Purgatorio*, which he cites, as *Lazarillo de Tormes*. The character he presents is that of the solitary, self-reliant rogue, at odds with society, improvising his life from day to day, accepting windfalls or hard knocks as they come. The narrative alternates between good luck and bad; the windfalls are usually sexual, the misfortunes his sufferings as an alienated individual. Since his luck is often good, it is hard to take his sufferings too seriously.

The first part of the book is devoted to Miller's experiences with the Cosmodemonic Telegraph Company. The subject gives him such momentum that the writing comes pouring out in a continuous torrential rush for the first fifty pages or so. After that the pace slows down somewhat to a continuous drift from one episode to another. After another fifty pages it has become more ebb and flow, without any discernible direction, carrying the flotsam and jetsam of the past. The monologue is like that of a garrulous old man with his mind out of focus, reminiscing endlessly, running on and on from one anecdote to another and another, interrupting himself, leaving parts unfinished, groping for some significance that was once there. But there are also some brilliant passages, like the long opening section and the famous Rabelaisian idyll in the middle. The critics who praise *Tropic of Capricorn* most highly remember its brilliance and forget the logorrhea.

During his years in Paris Miller wrote, in addition to his more famous narratives, enough expository prose to fill five volumes. His second book to be published, *Aller Retour New York* (1935), is set down in the form of a letter to his friend Alfred Perlès. It is a kind of travel book, begun in New York, where Miller had gone for a visit, continued aboard a Dutch ship, and completed in Paris. The epistolary form allows him ample freedom for description and comment: a picaresque tour of New York City during Prohibition, criticism of the American scene, ridicule of the stolid Dutch, relief upon his return to Paris.

Miller had always been a great letter writer, but this was his longest letter to date. It was soon dwarfed by his correspondence with Michael Fraenkel, begun in 1935, continued for three years, and eventually published as *Hamlet* (1939–43). Fraenkel, who appears in *Tropic of Cancer* as Boris, was a great talker who loved to engage Miller in endless philosophical discussions. They hit upon the scheme of writing out their ideas in letters to one another until they had written a book of exactly one thousand pages. Since they could argue on any topic, they arbitrarily agreed on a badly written work by a celebrity and settled on *Hamlet* in preference to *The Merry Widow*. Perlès, who was supposed to contribute, soon dropped out, unable to keep up the pace. But Miller and Fraenkel were inexhaustible. The correspondence is more like a conversation, or rather a debate, with long-winded alternating speeches. Miller's final letter runs to one hundred pages. Shake-speare's *Hamlet*, which was only a pretext, is soon forgotten, as the correspondence rambles in all directions. What gives it drama, as both must have realized, is the conflict between mind and spirit in the two characters: the systematic, cerebral, pessimistic philoso-pher and the mercurial, visceral, ebullient clown. Miller found the letter a congenial form, a written monologue, running on about the weather, ideas, books, recent experiences, all loosely linked by the amusing personality of the writer.

In addition to his books of the thirties, Miller wrote a number of miscellaneous pieces, usually for little magazines. A representa-tive sampling is to be found in his first collection, *Max and the White Phagocytes* (1938). Some of the material is familiar from his other books: a denunciation of American life reminiscent of *Aller Retour New York* and four letters from *Hamlet*. There are two narratives written in the vein of *Tropic of Cancer* and *Black Spring*: "Via Dieppe-Newhaven," an amusing account of an abor-tive trip to England where Miller was locked up as a suspicious character, and "Max," a character sketch of a Jewish refugee in Paris who is so low on the human scale that he begs from Miller. Written in 1935, "Max" is one of Miller's most perceptive works, a sardonic comment on the Christian treatment of Jews that is prophetic of impending horrors. What Max really begs for is sym-pathy, understanding, and recognition as a fellow human being. Miller, in an extraordinary mixture of compassion and ruthless-ness, dramatizes his own mixed feelings about this grotesque in-carnation of all human suffering. Max is at once comical and tragic, ludicrous, pathetic, and contemptible. But *Max and the White Phagocytes* is composed mainly of essays on art, literature, and the films. These present Miller in a new guise, as a critic.

As might be expected, his criticism reflects a good deal on his own work. In an essay on the painter Hans Reichel, "The Cosmological Eye," he admires the mystic perception akin to madness that produces visionary paintings. In "The Eye of Paris" he praises the photography of Brassai in terms that call to mind his own way of seeing Paris; most appropriately, Brassai's wonderful photographs of Paris nightlife, showing the prostitutes with their doll-like painted faces, were later used to illustrate *Quiet Days in Clichy*. In describing Anaïs Nin's diary, Miller shows how close his own confessions are to that form; his "Scenario," as a prefatory note explains, was inspired by one of her surrealist fantasies. In an essay on the art of the film, especially as practiced by Luis Buñuel, he appreciates a view of the world that is his own, both in its values and violence; the nightmare section of *Black Spring* — "Into the Night Life . . ." — resembles nothing so much as a film by Bunuel.

Miller makes an excellent critic of the visual arts. He has the years of appreciation, the understanding of the media, the taste, and the ability to express his vision that make a successful art critic. He is less successful as a literary critic. The two major literary essays in *Max and the White Phagocytes*, both provocative, nevertheless reveal certain limitations. "The Universe of Death" is part of a study of D. H. Lawrence that Miller struggled with for years, but never succeeded in finishing. He has explained that he was too close to Lawrence to see him objectively; the essay reveals other difficulties as well. What was supposed to be the last chapter of a book on Lawrence proves to be an attack on Proust and Joyce. In cursing them Miller seems to forget how close he is to them as a writer; much of his criticism reads like a rabid attack on the filth, stench, and corruption of Henry Miller. Of course Miller feels a far greater affinity for Lawrence; he too believes that writing should come from the solar plexus and not from the head. But the solar plexus is not the best portion of the anatomy for producing literary essays.

"An Open Letter to Surrealists Everywhere," though full of illuminating remarks, first shows up failings that are to characterize much of Miller's later writings: the tendency to harangue, the inability to sustain an argument, the facile generalization, and the free association of opinions. Basically Miller's trouble as an essayist stems from the fact that he is a man not of ideas but of attitudes. There is nothing wrong with this until he makes the mistake of choosing the wrong medium, using intellectual machinery to convey emotion. Generally he succeeds when he uses the essay for impressionistic description and appreciation, but not when he uses it to exhort or denounce.

Miller has produced four more miscellanies, if we count *The Cosmological Eye* (1939). His first book to be published in the United States, it reprints all but one of the selections from *Max and the White Phagocytes*, three sections of *Black Spring*, and three new pieces. The other three volumes are similar gatherings from various sources, including excerpts from works in progress or works never finished, such as his study of D. H. Lawrence. *The Wisdom of the Heart* (1941) is the best source for his reflections on philosophy and its expression in art, philosophy in a broad sense, embracing psychology and mysticism; the book includes two essays on Balzac, whose illuminism appealed profoundly to Miller. *Sunday after the War* (1944) is noteworthy for its three selections from *Sexus*, then unpublished, and for "Reunion in Brooklyn," that harrowing portrayal of his family, based on his observations after ten years' absence. *Stand Still like the Hummingbird* (1962) sweeps together a very uneven collection of essays, mostly on literary subjects.

In 1939, after the publication of *Tropic of Capricorn*, Miller decided to take a prolonged vacation. For years his good friend Lawrence Durrell had been inviting him to come to Greece. Miller had resisted the temptation, reluctant to break his working routine so long as *Tropic of Capricorn* was unfinished, but now he was free. After more than nine years in Paris he wanted to get away for a time and take a new perspective. He had worked hard during those years, he had completed his major projects, and he was ready for a complete change of scene and tempo. With a great sense of freedom and lightness he turned toward the Mediterranean world. A holiday spirit pervades Miller's account of his six months in Greece, *The Colossus of Maroussi* (1941). But his elation is somewhat sobered by the outbreak of war, which eventually forced him to return to America. The book was written in New York during the year following his visit to Greece. The mood of Greece was still upon him, and only intensified by his loathing of America and his feeling of being cut off.

The *Colossus of Maroussi* is one of Miller's finest books. The visit to Greece had been a high moment in his life, deeply affecting him in a number of ways. His account is much more than a travel book, though it is that too, dramatically conveying the spirit of place through the observer's personal intuitions. To Miller Greece was a holy land that aroused all his religious awe. On its bare rock men and gods had struggled and worshipped and left a record that could still be read. Miller's experience of the sacred places of Greece is deliberately unhistorical; what he wanted was not archaeology or history but a feeling of kinship with the men of the past. Significantly he began his trip to Greece by visiting the oldest region in France, the Dordogne Valley, whose caves bore testimony of the aesthetic and religious impulses of Cro-Magnon man. Disheartened by his own time, Miller preferred to take a millennial view of the human race.

Greece not only stirred antediluvial memories, it opened up several new worlds. It was both ancient and modern, with its pastoral landscape and Athens a blaze of electric lights. It was also an earthly Paradise. Always a city dweller, Miller had never before lived among the elements. In Greece the warm sea purged and rejuvenated him; Greece was a land of sun and sky and dazzling light; at night the astrologic world of the stars and planets was close at hand. But it was the Greeks themselves who most appealed to him. With their spontaneous warmth and their love of talk, they offered the kind of male comradeship he had been looking for all his life. The book is a record of great friendships and casual encounters with ordinary folk, with whom he communicated quite effectively by pantomime. The greatest character of all is his friend Katsimbalis, the colossus of the title, a man who grew larger than life when he talked, who poured enormous dramatic energies into his monologues. "I like the monologue even more than the duet, when it is good," Miller remarks. "It's like watching a man write a book expressly for you: he writes it, reads it aloud, acts it, revises it, savours it, enjoys it, enjoys your enjoyment of it, and then tears it up and throws it to the winds." Occasionally, inspired by Katsimbalis, Miller also performs. In fact, Katsimbalis is simply an alter ego, a man of similar talents, a manic, mythomanic, megalomanic character made in his own image.

Greece also brings out the Romantic enthusiast in Miller. He is in favor of all that is natural, free, and instinctive, unspoiled by civilization. He likes haggling and takes delight in being cheated by transparently wily Greeks. He prefers the slums at its base to the Acropolis itself, the murderer to the corporation executive, shabby old hotels to modern comforts. His antipathies are just as explicit as his sympathies, and his cantankerous crotchets just as Romantic: "I don't like jails, churches, fortresses, palaces, libraries, museums, nor public statues to the dead." In Greece he turns his back on France with its rational, controlled, ordered way of life; in fact he renounces all of Western civilization. And he is most intolerant of the Americanized Greeks he meets everywhere he goes, who appreciate the worst of American materialism and noth-

34

ing of their own culture. Underlying many of his attitudes is the war, the final proof that the modern world is dehumanized and death-driven.

The same attitudes pervade another travel book, *The Air-Conditioned Nightmare* (1945). When Miller returned from his ten years in Europe he decided to tour the United States and record his impressions as he went. He spent a year zigzagging across the country and back. His account of the journey is as erratic as his route. It would hardly serve as a guide to the United States, but it provides a good index to Miller's opinions. Chiefly he is appalled by his native land. The country is magnificent, but the people are dead, all but the Negroes, Indians, and an occasional nonconformist. The American way of life has created a spiritual and cultural wasteland, with its obsession for objects and money, its modern conveniences, advertising, radio programs, movies, comic strips, battleships, bombs, vitamins, canned foods. "Why is it that in America the great works of art are all Nature's doing? There were the skyscrapers, to be sure, and the dams and bridges and the concrete highways. All utilitarian. Nowhere in America was there anything comparable to the cathedrals of Europe, the temples of Asia and Egypt — enduring monuments created out of faith and love and passion. No exaltation, no fervor, no zeal — except to increase business, facilitate transportation, enlarge the domain of ruthless exploitation."

For all its anathemas, *The Air-Conditioned Nightmare* is a thoroughly American book. Miller rages *because* he is truly American, because he believes in the national ideal with a fundamentalist fervor. The book is very American in flavor. Miller is in love with American names, adept at catching the American idiom, and most in sympathy with the American characters he singles out: cranks and dreamers, shrewd homespun individualists or just plain folks. The very notion of a transcontinental odyssey is in the best native tradition, with unexpected adventures and excursions off the beaten track a part of the pattern. Miller is a burlesque pioneer, a helplessly inept mechanic at the mercy of glib repairmen and his secondhand Buick; "Automotive Passacaglia" recounts his vicissitudes with that temperamental machine. Poor eyesight makes his journey as hazardous as that of the early settlers, and he captures some of westering drive in crossing the endless miles of hot, barren landscape — only to find in southern California everything he loathes. His report of that exhausting drive, "From Grand Canyon to Burbank," is immediately followed by an account of his first evening upon arrival, "Soirée in Hollywood," a satire on besotted, aggressive, wealthy Americanism. The shift in tempo, tone, and setting could not be more striking. Taken together, the two recapitulate the western course of empire from the pioneering journey to the corruption of the Promised Land.

Originally Miller planned to write two volumes of *The Air-Conditioned Nightmare*, but like many of his projects, this one had a way of changing as it went along. The second volume, *Remember to Remember* (1947), is a sequel only in the sense that it presents the same man airing similar opinions. Both volumes are miscellaneous collections of sketches. The second is built around persons rather than places, for Miller's travels had ended in 1944, when he settled in Big Sur. Here again, as in the earlier volume, he makes a point of discovering unsung genius and prefers to believe that the genuine artist is always unrecognized. The book is prefaced by a long political sermon on the state of the post-atomic world and contains another three times as long which repeats many of the same views. Henry Miller on war and peace sometimes sounds like Henry David Thoreau, but often lacks the common sense and is often shrill. The best parts of the book are his reminiscences of France in the title essay; "Astrological Fricassee," another Hollywood party where the conversation brilliantly carries the satire; and "The Staff of Life," a humorous essay on the tasteless, colorless, odorless, soulless white bread that sums up what is wrong with the United States.

Apart from his book on Greece and his two books on America, during the forties Miller devoted himself mostly to his confessions. In 1940 he wrote two short books containing some autobiographical elements, *The World of Sex* and *Quiet Days in Clichy*. In 1941–42 he began work on his long, slightly fictionalized autobiography, *The Rosy Crucifixion*, writing the part that was published as *Sexus* in 1949; he revised *Sexus* several times as he moved from New York to Los Angeles to Big Sur. In 1947 he began writing the second part, *Plexus*. Again there was a considerable delay before publication; *Plexus* first appeared in French in 1952. The third part, *Nexus*, was written some ten years later, only appearing in 1960; at that time it was labeled "Volume I," and Miller still intends to write a second volume. All of these books are more or less obscene and could not be published openly in this country at the time they were written. *The World of Sex* was published in a limited edition in 1940 by Ben Abramson of the Argus Book Shop in Chicago; the others did not appear in American editions until 1965.

Quiet Days in Clichy, as the title suggests, narrates personal experiences of the early thirties when Miller was living in Clichy with his friend Perlès. The material is like that in *Tropic of Cancer,* but the book seems to have been written by a different man. It is good storytelling and realistic reporting, but it has none of the vehemence that made the earlier book a cry of passionate protest and none of the "ecstasy," none of the heightened subjective vision that informed the earlier writing. The explanation may lie in the fact that the manuscript disappeared from sight for fifteen years and Miller rewrote it for publication in 1956. In the thirties his writing was always elated, euphoric, airborne; in the fifties, his prose became more pedestrian.

The World of Sex was also rewritten. In 1957, when Olympia Press decided to publish it in Paris, Miller revised the text extensively. The second version adds nothing to the first, and often takes the bite out of incisive passages with fussy alterations. By 1957, Miller was a different man; he had assumed his Big Sur mantle and was addressing an audience. In 1940, he was merely trying to clarify some of his ideas and did not care if no one listened. *The World of Sex* is his *biographia literaria*, a key statement that defines the role of sex in his writings and in his life. Written at midpoint in his career as a kind of postscript to *Tropic of Capricorn*, it serves to explain his purpose in that book and to introduce the other autobiographical volumes that are to follow.

Sexus, *Plexus*, and *Nexus*, taken together, are simply an enormously expanded *Tropic of Capricorn*. All these books deal with Miller's life during the twenties when he was trying to discover himself. This is the central story that he has been trying to tell ever since 1932, when he started writing *Tropic of Capricorn*, the story of his "rosy crucifixion," when he died as an ordinary mortal and was resurrected as a writer. Originally he thought he could explain the miracle in one volume. It took him five or six years to finish *Tropic of Capricorn*, only to discover that the mystery had eluded him. The events he narrated were in some mysterious way deeply significant to him, yet he had not succeeded in explaining the significance even to himself. In the Coda he admits that he has lost the way: "I wander aimlessly, trying to gain a solid, unshakable foothold whence I can command a view of my life, but behind me there lies only a welter of crisscrossed tracks, a groping, confused, encircling, the spasmodic gambit of the chicken whose head has just been lopped off." This statement applies even more to the subsequent volumes. The three parts of *The Rosy*

Crucifixion cover the same ground much more exhaustively, yet the point seems to recede farther and farther all the time. The mystery is intertwined somehow with the great love of his life, which coincided with his metamorphosis. Mona or Mara, as she is called, seems to embody the mystery. *Tropic of Capricorn* was dedicated "To Her," though she did not figure much in that book. She is the principal character of the later volumes, but still she remains something of an enigma, mysterious in her origins, elusive and devious in her ways. Somewhat hysterical, apparently a pathological liar, perhaps a Lesbian, she nevertheless continues to fascinate Miller and represents for him the eternal inscrutable feminine. Whatever her character, Mona played a crucial role in Miller's self-realization. She prevailed upon him to quit his job and practically forced him to write. She was also determined that he go to Europe, and, as Miller tells the story in *Nexus*, found a patron who paid her for Miller's writing. The trilogy spans the period between 1923, when he first met her in a dance hall, and 1928, when they were about to sail for Europe.

Miller's method is rather like psychoanalysis. He seems to be putting down everything he can remember about the period, in hopes that some meaning will ultimately emerge from the mass. He claims to be writing according to a plan that was "dictated" to him in 1927, and he hopes to isolate the crucial moments of his life, but the writing gives the impression of having been put down at random, as it occurred to him in reminiscence, and never edited. A great deal of space is given to his early friends, his experiences and conversations with them, largely pointless except that they feel he is destined to become a writer. To him the most significant acquaintances are Russian Jews, who bring to life the world of his idol, Dostoevski, and who exude a rich and ancient culture. Miller wants to become a Jew, wants to escape the respectable, bourgeois, Gentile America of his birth.

As might be expected, the three volumes of the trilogy differ considerably. *Sexus* is the most obscene of all Miller's works, and the sexual episodes, which alternate regularly with neutral passages, often seem gratuitous. The other two volumes contain hardly any obscenity. *Sexus* is also the most disorganized, with constant digressions, reminiscences, and other excursions interrupting the main thread. In *Plexus* and *Nexus* the narrative becomes more factual and straightforward, and as a result offers a clearer explanation of Miller's emergence from his past. The writing also grows progressively easier and more natural. Only *Nexus* deals much with Miller's efforts to write. His chief concern in *Sexus* is fornication, and in *Plexus*, surprisingly, is making money. The whole trilogy reports some unlikely ventures, with Miller running a speakeasy, selling encyclopedias, hitchhiking to Florida to get in on the real estate boom, grave-digging, even psychoanalyzing a psychoanalyst friend. The first two volumes, though redeemed by occasional virtuoso passages, are far too long. Miller as always is good at evoking scenes, the more squalid the better. The most vivid passages in *Sexus* are a description of the East Side ghetto and another of a church in Naples. *Plexus* retails some wonderful dreams and several good stories. But there is a great deal of weary plodding between such passages. *The Rosy Crucifixion* is four times as long as *Tropic of Capricorn*, with little of the humor, ferocity, or pyrotechnics.

During his years at Big Sur Miller's writing deteriorated, often becoming what he had revolted against in the thirties, "literary" in the bad sense, inflated with subjunctives, rhetorical questions, and exclamations. He lapsed into a fatal facility, writing more and more about less and less, quoting clichés as though they were choice aphorisms. Success did him no good. As his fame increased, all kinds of people came to Big Sur on pilgrimage to visit the Sage, and many more wrote fervent letters. "Henry has as many fans as

40

a movie star," Alfred Perlès noted in *My Friend, Henry Miller,* finished at Big Sur. As he became a famous personage, Miller made the mistake of taking himself too seriously. His later essays are solemn and pontifical, as he addresses the faithful.

The Books in My Life (1952) is embarrassingly egocentric. Written at the request of his friend Lawrence Clark Powell, the librarian who supplied him with books, it is not the interesting record of an autodidact's education it could have been, but a laundry list. Miller considers everything that happens to him momentous, not only in the past but even in the future. In addition to an appendix listing the hundred books that influenced him most there is one listing the books he still intends to read. In short, he has lost his sense of humor and his sense of balance. There is too much Rider Haggard here, not enough Lao-tse. The book is mainly about the late nineteenth-century romances he read as a boy and does not come to grips with the writers who influenced him as a man. Of course he has every reason to include his boyhood reading, but as he rereads that Victorian prose, he falls under its spell and lapses into the same stilted, pseudo-archaic language which no man ever spoke, the same melodramatic and platitudinous sentiments. "Ah, there's the miracle! Whoso has the power to affect us more and more deeply each time we read him is indeed a master, no matter what his name, rank or status be." Written immediately after *Plexus, The Books in My Life* betrays what is wrong with *The Rosy Crucifixion*: Miller's model is Rider Haggard's *She.*

Miller's book about Rimbaud tells more about that writer's effect on him, though Rimbaud was not a formative influence like Dostoevski or Whitman. Miller became absorbed in Rimbaud long after he was an established writer himself. In 1943 he undertook to render *A Season in Hell* into a comparable American idiom, but he finally gave up the attempt and wrote instead two long essays on Rimbaud. These first appeared in the New Directions anthologies of 1946 and 1949 and were eventually published as a book, *The Time of the Assassins* (1956). Despite its subtitle, this is not really a study of Rimbaud, but a collection of rambling reflections on his life and character, in which Miller finds astonishing parallels to his own. Though rather megalomaniacal, the book does show a relation between the two — not in their destinies, as Miller likes to imagine, but in their Romantic agonizing. The book also shows Miller's affinity for other anguished spirits of the late nineteenth century and places him squarely in the late Romantic tradition. The Coda tells more in a few pages than all the discursive ruminations of *The Books in My Life*.

Big Sur and the Oranges of Hieronymus Bosch (1957) presents Miller's meditations from his own particular Walden. The idyllic setting of Big Sur quite naturally brought to mind Thoreau, the American frontier, and Utopian communities. But by the time he wrote about it, Miller's life there was anything but serene. Shortly after moving to Big Sur, he had married for the third time, but this marriage had broken up and his wife had left him with two small children to look after. In 1953 he married for the fourth time and was relieved of some of his child-rearing duties. But every year brought more admirers to Big Sur. Harried by visitors, correspondence, and household chores, he could scarcely find time to write. As a result his writing is more distracted than ever. "Where was I?" he keeps asking himself, trying to pick up the thread of an essay. Quite rightly he calls the main body of the book "A Potpourri." He ranges here from amusing storytelling to long-winded preaching, demonstrating once again that he is best as a storyteller, worst when philosophizing. The best section of the book is the self-contained narrative that was published separately the previous year as *A Devil in Paradise*. It tells the story of his acquaintance with Conrad Moricand, an astrologer

Miller had known in Paris and made the mistake of inviting to Big Sur, only to be imposed on outrageously.

Miller's life in Big Sur finally became too complicated, and in 1960 he left. In a sense he came back down to earth, but he has written little since. For a year he traveled about Europe, lionized by writers and publishers. Then he retired to southern California, where he has found a relatively peaceful life and devoted himself to an art he has always loved, painting watercolors. He has often said in his later years that when he had finished his life's work, *The Rosy Crucifixion*, he would turn to nonsense and slapstick; and at the age of seventy he finished his first play, *Just Wild about Harry* (1963), a mixture of vaudeville, melodrama, and musical comedy, filled with popular songs from his entire lifetime. Apart from this, all of his writing published in recent years belongs to the past. Several selections of his work have appeared, of which by far the most comprehensive is *The Henry Miller Reader*, edited by Lawrence Durrell with Miller's running commentary. Two volumes of letters have been published, one selected from his abundant and lively correspondence with Durrell over a quarter of a century, the other a selection of Miller's letters to Anaïs Nin, which tells much about his most creative years, 1931 to 1946.

In recent years, with the publication of his banned books, Miller has been more than ever in the news. Now that these have appeared, almost all of his writings are in print, and mostly in paperback. Gradually a calmer view of his work is emerging, not only in the public mind but among literary historians. His final place has yet to be determined, but he is being generally recognized as one of the important writers of his time, one of the most expressive of the thirties, and certainly the best surrealist writer America has produced. And while it is hard to imagine that the *Tropics* will ever be taught in the schools, several of his books should occupy a lasting place in American literature.

The bibliography of Henry Miller is somewhat confused by expatriate publication, amateur enterprises, and other unusual circumstances. Two of his books were first published in translation. Some works appeared independently and were later incorporated into others; for example, *A Devil in Paradise* (1956) became part of *Big Sur and the Oranges of Hieronymus Bosch* (1957). A number of essays were first published in pamphlet form and later collected in miscellanies, such as *Money and How It Gets That Way* (1938), anthologized many years later in *Stand Still like the Hummingbird* (1962). Some pamphlets reprint excerpts from already published works; some are merely advertising brochures. To clarify the record, the list below gives only the first edition in English and only pamphlets containing material which does not appear elsewhere.

Works of Henry Miller

Tropic of Cancer. Paris: Obelisk Press, 1934.
What Are You Going to Do about Alf? Paris: printed at author's expense, 1935.
Aller Retour New York. Paris: Obelisk Press, 1935.
Black Spring. Paris: Obelisk Press, 1936.
Max and the White Phagocytes. Paris: Obelisk Press, 1938.
Tropic of Capricorn. Paris: Obelisk Press, 1939.
Hamlet (with Michael Fraenkel). Vol. I, Santurce, Puerto Rico: Carrefour, 1939. Vol. II, New York: Carrefour, 1941. Vol. I complete, New York: Carrefour, 1943.
The Cosmological Eye. New York: New Directions, 1939.
The World of Sex. [Chicago: Ben Abramson, Argus Book Shop, 1940.]
The Colossus of Maroussi. San Francisco: Colt Press, 1941.
The Wisdom of the Heart. New York: New Directions, 1941.
Sunday after the War. New York: New Directions, 1944.
Semblance of a Devoted Past. Berkeley, Calif.: Bern Porter, 1944.
The Plight of the Creative Artist in the United States of America. Houlton, Me.: Bern Porter, 1944.
Echolalia. Berkeley, Calif.: Bern Porter, 1945.
Henry Miller Miscellanea. San Mateo, Calif.: Bern Porter, 1945.
Why Abstract? (with Hilaire Hiler and William Saroyan). New York: New Directions, 1945.

44

The Air-Conditioned Nightmare. New York: New Directions, 1945.
Maurizius Forever. San Francisco: Colt Press, 1946.
Remember to Remember. New York: New Directions, 1947.
The Smile at the Foot of the Ladder. New York: Duell, Sloan, and Pearce, 1948.
Sexus (Book One of *The Rosy Crucifixion*). Paris: Obelisk Press, 1949.
The Waters Reglitterized. San Jose, Calif.: John Kidis, 1950.
The Books in My Life. New York: New Directions, 1952.
Plexus (Book Two of *The Rosy Crucifixion*). Paris: Olympia Press, 1953.
Quiet Days in Clichy. Paris: Olympia Press, 1956.
The Time of the Assassins: A Study of Rimbaud. New York: New Directions, 1956.
Big Sur and the Oranges of Hieronymus Bosch. New York: New Directions, 1957.
The Red Notebook. Highlands, N.C.: Jonathan Williams, 1958.
Reunion in Barcelona. Northwood, England: Scorpion Press, 1959.
Nexus (Book Three of *The Rosy Crucifixion*). Paris: Obelisk Press, 1960.
To Paint Is to Love Again. Alhambra, Calif.: Cambria Books, 1960.
Watercolors, Drawings, and His Essay, "The Angel Is My Watermark." New York: Abrams, 1962.
Stand Still like the Hummingbird. New York: New Directions, 1962.
Just Wild about Harry. New York: New Directions, 1963.
Greece (with drawings by Anne Poor). New York: Viking Press, 1964.

Writings Edited by Others

Nights of Love and Laughter, with an introduction by Kenneth Rexroth. New York: Signet, 1955.
The Intimate Henry Miller, with an introduction by Lawrence Clark Powell. New York: Signet, 1959.
The Henry Miller Reader, edited by Lawrence Durrell. New York: New Directions, 1959.
Lawrence Durrell and Henry Miller: A Private Correspondence, edited by George Wickes. New York: Dutton, 1963.
Henry Miller on Writing, edited by Thomas H. Moore. New York: New Directions, 1964.
Henry Miller, Letters to Anaïs Nin, edited by Gunther Stuhlmann. New York: Putnam, 1965.

Current American Reprints

The Air-Conditioned Nightmare. New York: Avon. $.75.
Big Sur and the Oranges of Hieronymus Bosch. New York: New Directions. $2.50.

Black Spring. New York: Evergreen Black Cat Series (Grove Press). $.95.
The Colossus of Maroussi. New York: New Directions. $1.55.
The Cosmological Eye. New York: New Directions. $1.75.
Nexus. New York: Evergreen Black Cat Series. $.95.
Plexus. New York: Evergreen Black Cat Series. $1.25.
Quiet Days in Clichy. New York: Evergreen Black Cat Series. $.75.
Remember to Remember. New York: New Directions. $1.95.
Sexus. New York: Evergreen Black Cat Series. $1.25.
Sunday after the War. New York: New Directions. $1.65.
The Time of the Assassins. New York: New Directions. $1.40.
Tropic of Cancer. New York: Evergreen Black Cat Series. $.95.
Tropic of Capricorn. New York: Evergreen Black Cat Series. $2.45.
The Wisdom of the Heart. New York: New Directions. $1.45.
The World of Sex. New York: Evergreen Black Cat Series. $.75.

Bibliographies

Moore, Thomas H. *Bibliography of Henry Miller.* Minneapolis: Henry Miller Literary Society, 1961.
Renken, Maxine. *A Bibliography of Henry Miller, 1945–1961.* Denver: Alan Swallow, 1962.
Riley, Esta Lou. *Henry Miller, An Informal Bibliography, 1924–1960.* Hays, Kans.: Fort Hays Kansas State College, 1961.

Critical and Biographical Studies

Baxter, Annette Kar. *Henry Miller, Expatriate.* Pittsburgh: University of Pittsburgh Press, 1961.
Durrell, Lawrence, and Alfred Perlès. *Art and Outrage.* London: Putnam, 1959.
Hassan, Ihab. *Samuel Beckett and Henry Miller: Two Modes of the Avant-Garde.* New York: Random House, forthcoming.
Perlès, Alfred. *My Friend, Henry Miller.* London: Neville Spearman, 1955.
Porter, Bern, editor. *The Happy Rock.* Berkeley, Calif.: Bern Porter, 1945.
Wickes, George, editor. *Henry Miller and the Critics.* Carbondale, Ill.: Southern Illinois University Press, 1963.
———, interviewer. "Henry Miller," in *Writers at Work: The Paris Review Interviews, Second Series.* New York: Viking, 1963.
Widmer, Kingsley. *Henry Miller.* New York: Twayne, 1963.